The month of April, from the illuminated manuscript
Les Très Riches Heures du duc de Berry

The Story of a Special Day
Volume 102

April 11

101st day of the year
(102nd in leap years)
264 days remaining
until the end of the year.

by Michael Dobson

Timespinner Press

Table of Contents

Cover: Liftoff of Apollo 13, April 11, 1970, the Event of the Day.

Back Cover and Frontispiece: The month of April, from the French Gothic illuminated manuscript *Les Très Riches Heures du duc de Berry.*

April 11 Quotations

"I fired him because he wouldn't respect the authority of the president. That's the answer to that. I didn't fire him because he was a dumb son of a bitch, although he was, but that's not against the law for generals. If it was, half to three-quarters of them would be in jail."

> —*President Harry S. Truman on the April 11, 1951, firing of General Douglas MacArthur*

"A man has to live with himself, and he should see to it that he always has good company."

> —*Chief Justice Charles Evans Hughes, born April 11, 1862*

"Every passing hour brings the Solar System forty-three thousand miles closer to Globular Cluster M13 in Hercules — and still there are some misfits who insist that there is no such thing as progress."

> —*Kurt Vonnegut, died April 11, 2007*

"Nothing can be said: nothing sure, nothing probable, nothing honest. Better to err through omission than through commission: better to refrain from steering the fate of others, since it is already so difficult to navigate one's own."

> —*Primo Levi, died April 11, 1987*

Event of the Day
Apollo 13 Lifts Off!

Apollo 13 Mission Insignia

Although the United States officially "won" the space race with Apollo 11 on July 20, 1969, there would be five more missions to the Moon, during four of which astronauts walked on the lunar surface. The exception was Apollo 13, the seventh manned mission in the program.

On April 13, 1970, at 13:13 Central Standard time, James A. Lovell Jr., John L. Swigert Jr., and Fred W. Haise Jr. lifted off on their mission to the moon. About 56 hours after takeoff, there was a loud bang. Number 2 oxygen tank had exploded.

Over the next two hours, the entire oxygen supply of the service module was lost. The command module was left with backup battery power only.

The crippled Apollo 13 command module, showing the damage

Landing on the Moon was no longer an option, and there were many obstacles to be overcome so that the Apollo 13 crew could return to Earth. First, they had to make a course correction so they could use the Moon's gravity as a slingshot, requiring Jim Lovell to fly the spacecraft using only the sun in the cockpit window as an alignment star.

While there was plenty of oxygen in the lunar module, carbon dioxide removal required the use of lithium hydroxide canisters. An engineering team created a kludged-together system using plastic bags, cardboard, and tape to adapt canisters made for the command module for use in the LM.

Power supplies, water, and food were limited. The crew became dehydrated; Lovell lost 14 pounds.

The team managed to overcome one problem after another, but the toughest technical challenge came at the end of the mission. There had never been a case where the command module had to be powered up after a long sleep, and the flight controllers had to test and write new procedures to accomplish it, doing three months' work in three days. Even worse, by the time the Apollo 13 team reentered the command module, condensation had covered the interior with fine droplets of water. Water was inside the circuit panels as well, and the chance of a short circuit was all too real. Fortunately, safeguards against short circuits installed in the aftermath of Apollo 1 worked as planned.

As they entered the atmosphere, the heat of reentry created rain inside the command module. But that was the final hazard. On April 17, 1970, Apollo 13 splashed down safely near American Samoa.

April 11 Holidays and Celebrations

Juan Santamaría Day (Costa Rica)

Juan Santamaría Day commemorates the death of the Costa Rican national hero Juan Santamaría in a war against American lawyer William Walker, who had organized a private military expedition that overthrew Nicaragua's government and sought to take over other Central American countries to form a slave-holding empire under his personal control. (This practice was known as "filibustering," which later gave its name to the U.S. Senate process.)

Santamaría, a poor illegitimate son of a single mother, joined the Costa Rican army as a drummer boy. During the Second Battle of Rivas on April 11, 1856, Costa Rican troops tried to take a building used by Walker's men as a fortress and sniper perch. Santamaría volunteered to set the building on fire on the condition that if he died, someone would look after his mother. He succeeded in setting fire to the building, but was mortally wounded in the process.

In addition to the national holiday in his honor, Santamaría is commemorated with statues. His mother was awarded his military pension.

Easter Season

Easter is a "moveable feast," meaning it occurs on different days each year. In Western Christianity, Easter can occur anywhere between March 22 and April 25; in Eastern Christianity it can occur anywhere from April 4 to May 8. (The difference is that Eastern Christianity calculates according to the older Julian calendar rather than the modern Gregorian calendar. See "What Day of the Week is April 11?" for an explanation.) All events of the Easter season adjust accordingly. See the "Easter Events" section for more details.

Christian Feast Days

In **Western Christianity**, April 11 is the feast day of Antipas of Pergamum, Gemma Galgani, Godeberta, Guthlac, and Stanislaus of Szczezpanów.

In **Eastern Orthodox Christianity**, April 11 is also the commemoration of Antipas, along with Saint Pharmuthius, Saint Processus and Martinian of Rome, Saint John the disciple of Saint Gregory, Saint James of Zheleznoborov, Saints Euthymius and Chariton of Syanzhemsk, Saint Barsanuphius of Tver, and Saint Callinicus of Cernica. (These events are observed on April 24 by "Old Calendarists" who use the Julian calendar.)

What Happened on April 11?

1689 CE – **William and Mary Are Crowned**

Following the Glorious Revolution that deposed King James II and VII, the prince of Orange-Nassau, William III, and his wife Mary II (left; painting by Sir James Thornhill), were crowned King and Queen of England on April 11, 1689. They ruled jointly until Mary's death in 1694; William III continued on the throne until 1702. The reign of William and Mary was an important transition between the personal rule of the Stuart line to the more Parliament-centered rule of subsequent British monarchs.

1713 CE – **The Treaty of Utrecht is Signed**

The Treaty of Utrecht, signed April 11, 1713, ended the War of the Spanish Succession over who should succeed Charles II as King of Spain. The war had raged since 1701, and involved Spain, Great Britain, France, Portugal, Savoy, and the Dutch Republic. While it took place mostly in Europe, it included Queen Anne's War in North America. The war placed the French candidate, Philip IV, on the Spanish throne, but only on the condition that he renounce his claim to the French throne — preventing a union of France and Spain under the same throne was the principal reason for the war.

1814 CE – **Napoleon is Exiled to Elba**

The War of the Sixth Coalition pitted the armies of Austria, Prussia, Russia, Sweden, the United Kingdom, Spain, Portugal, and various small German states against the forces of French Emperor Napoléon Bonaparte.

Napoléon Bonaparte by Paul Delaroche

By 1814, they had occupied Paris, and negotiated the Treaty of Fontainebleau, which removed Napoléon as Emperor of France and sent him into exile on the island of Elba. Less than a year later, Napoléon would escape Elba and return for what became known as the Hundred Days, ending with Napoléon's defeat at the Battle of Waterloo and his exile to St. Helena, where he remained until his death in 1821.

1869 CE – **End of the Shogunate**

From 1600 to 1868, the Tokugawa Shogunate (徳川幕府), a feudal government, ruled Japan. The 15th and last shogun, Tokugawa Yoshinobu (徳川 慶喜), fought against a rising rebellion in the Boshin War. In 1868, Yoshinobu decided to place himself under voluntary confinement and submit himself to the imperial court rather that continue the war, even though his forced outnumbered the opposition. On April 11, 1869, he handed over Edo Castle to the imperial army, sparing Tokyo from war. He spent the rest of his life in retirement, participating in numerous hobbies, including photography and painting. He was restored to the rank of prince in 1902 for his loyal service to Japan, and died in 193.

1881 CE – **Founding of Spelman College**

Known originally as the Atlanta Baptst Female Seminary, Spelman College was the fourth historically black female institution of higher education to be chartered as a college in the United States. Of the three earlier institutions, Scotia Seminar merged with Barber Memorial College, Mount Hermon Female Seminary closed in 1924, and Bennett College in Greensboro, North Carolina opened as a co-educational facility and became a women's college in 1926. It has produced a number of famous alumni, including Marian Wright Edelman, Keshia Knight Pulliam, Esther Rolle, and Alice Walker.

1921 CE – **Establishment of Transjordan**

The Emirate of Transjordan (إمارة شرق الأردن), a British protectorate, came out of the Cairo Conference of 1921 as part of the British Mandate for Palestine. It divided the area controlled by Britain along the Jordan River, with one side become Palestine and the other Transjordan. The Hashemite ruler Abdullah I (عبد الله الأول بن الحسين) established a government for the emirate on April 11, 1921. He would be emir until independence in 1949, at which time he became king of the Hashemite Kingdom of Transjordan, later simply Jordan.

1945 CE – **Liberation of Buchenwald**

On the afternoon of April 11, 1945, troops of the U.S. 9th Armored Infantry Battalion, part of Patton's Third Army, entered Buchenwald Concentration Camp, liberating it from the Nazis, most of whom had already fled. Buchenwald, along with several of its subcamps, was the first concentration camp liberated by U.S. forces. Photographs of the prisoners shocked the world, and formed one of the first concrete and specific images of what became known as the Holocaust.

A Buchenwald survivor identifies a Nazi guard

1951 CE – **Douglas MacArthur is Fired**

After making repeated public statements contradicting and opposing the policies of President Harry S. Truman, General Douglas MacArthur was relieved of command by the President on April 11, 1951. This was a politically explosive move, causing Truman's popularity ratings to plummet.

MacArthur's relationship with FDR had also been tempestuous, and he had nearly been removed from command before. The firing reestablished the principle of civilian control of the U.S. military.

Douglas MacArthur upon returning to the United States

1951 CE – **The Stone of Scone is Recovered**

The Stone of Scone, also known as the Stone of Destiny or the Coronation Stone, has been used for centuries as part of the coronation of the monarch of Scotland, and with the union of Scotland and England, for the coronation of monarchs of Great Britain.

It was stolen from Westminster Abbey by four Scottish students on Christmas Day 1950, and a massive police hunt resulted. The students left the stone on the altar at Arborath Abbey in Scotland on April 11, 1954. The abbots informed London police, and the stone, which had been accidentally broken during the theft, was returned to Westminster Abbey.

1954 CE – Most Boring Day Since 1900

After compiling over 300 million facts about people, places, businesses, events, and other matters, the computer program True Knowledge, developed by Cambridge scientist William Tunstall-Pedoe, announced in 2010 that nothing of note happened on April 11, 1954, making it the most boring day of of the 20th century.

1961 CE – Trial of Adolf Eichmann Beings

Nazi SS Lieutenant Colonel Adolf Eichmann headed the Central Office for Jewish Emigration, which organized and oversaw concentration and death camps, the expropriation of Jewish proprty, and the deportation of Jews.

Following the infamous Wannsee Conference in which the "final solution to the Jewish question" was decided by the Nazi leadership, he was made Transportation Administrator, responsible for the logistics of the Holocaust.

After the war, he managed to hide his true identity from U.S. interrogators, escaped custody, and eventually reached Argentina, where he hid successfully until 1960, when he was captured by the Israeli intelligence organization Mossad and brought to Israel to stand trial.

The trial itself, which began on April 11, 1961, resulted in international controversy, as it was feared Eichmann's testimony would implicate many others, including Germans brought to the United States and former Nazis serving in the German government. Eichmann was sentenced death and hanged on May 31, 1962.

1968 CE – **LBJ Signs the Civil Rights Act of 1968**

The three major pieces of civil rights legislation that dismantled legal apartheid in the United States were the Civil Rights Act of 1964, outlawing most forms of discrimination, the Voting Rights Act of 1965, outlawing various practices that disenfranchised African-Americans, and finally the Civil Rights Act of 1968, prohibiting discrimination in housing. That bill was passed by Congress on April 10, 1968, and signed into law by President Lyndon B. Johnson the following day.

LBJ signs the Civil Rights Act of 1968

1976 CE – **First Apple Computer**

The first product of the Apple Computer Company was the Apple-1, designed and hand-built by Steve Wozniak and sold by Steve Jobs. About 200 units in total were produced.

Unlike other early personal computers, the Apple-1 came fully assembled — although without a case, a power supply transformer, a power switch, a keyboard, or a display. It sold for $666.66, because Wozniak liked repeating digits and the wholesale price was $500.

Apple Introduces the First Low Cost Microcomputer System with a Video Terminal and 8K Bytes of RAM on a Single PC Card.

The Apple Computer. A truly complete microcomputer system on a single PC board. Based on the MOS Technology 6502 microprocessor, the Apple also has a built-in video terminal and sockets for 8K bytes of onboard RAM memory. With the addition of a keyboard and video monitor, you'll have an extremely powerful computer system that can be used for anything from developing programs to playing games or running BASIC.

Combining the computer, video terminal and dynamic memory on a single board has resulted in a large reduction in chip count, which means more reliability and lowered cost. Since the Apple comes fully assembled, tested & burned-in and has a complete power supply on-board, initial set-up is essentially "hassle free" and you can be running within minutes. At $666.66 (including 4K bytes RAM!) it opens many new possibilities for users and systems manufacturers.

You Don't Need an Expensive Teletype.

Using the built-in video terminal and keyboard interface, you avoid all the expense, noise and maintenance associated with a teletype. And the Apple video terminal is six times faster than a teletype, which means more throughput and less waiting. The Apple connects directly to a video monitor (or home TV with an inexpensive RF modulator) and displays 960 easy to read characters in 24 rows of 40 characters per line with automatic scrolling. The video display section contains its own 1K bytes of memory, so all the RAM memory is available for user programs. And the Keyboard Interface lets you use almost any ASCII-encoded keyboard.

The Apple Computer makes it possible for many people with limited budgets to step up to a video terminal as an I/O device for their computer.

No More Switches, No More Lights.

Compared to switches and LED's, a video terminal can display vast amounts of information simultaneously. The Apple video terminal can display the contents of 192 memory locations at once on the screen. And the firmware in PROMS enables you to enter, display and debug programs (all in hex) from the keyboard, rendering a front panel unnecessary. The firmware also allows your programs to print characters on the display, and since you'll be looking at letters and numbers instead of just LED's, the door is open to all kinds of alphanumeric software (i.e., Games and BASIC).

8K Bytes RAM in 16 Chips!

The Apple Computer uses the new 16-pin 4K dynamic memory chips. They are faster and take ¼ the space and power of even the low power 2102's (the memory chip that everyone else uses). That means 8K bytes in sixteen chips. It also means no more 28 amp power supplies.

The system is fully expandable to 65K via an edge connector which carries both the address and data busses. All dynamic memory refreshing for both on and off-board memory is done automatically. Also, the Apple Computer can be upgraded to use the 16K chips when they become available. That's 32K bytes on-board RAM in 16 IC's—the equivalent of 256 2102's!

A Little Cassette Board That Works!

Unlike many other cassette boards on the marketplace, ours works every time. It plugs directly into the upright connector on the main board and stands only 2" tall. And since it is very fast (1500 bits per second), you can read or write 4K bytes in about 20 seconds. All timing is done in software, which results in crystal-controlled accuracy and uniformity from unit to unit.

Unlike some other cassette interfaces which require an expensive tape recorder, the Apple Cassette Interface works reliably with almost any audio-grade cassette recorder.

Software:

A tape of **APPLE BASIC** is included free with the Cassette Interface. Apple Basic features immediate error messages and fast execution, and lets you program in a higher level language immediately and without added cost. Also available **now** are a dis-assembler and many games, with many software packages, (including a macro assembler) in the works. And since our philosophy is to provide software for our machines free or at minimal cost, you won't be continually paying for access to this growing software library.

The Apple Computer is in stock at almost all major computer stores. (If your local computer store doesn't carry our products, encourage them or write us direct). **Dealer inquiries invited.**

Byte into an Apple $666.66*
* includes 4K bytes RAM

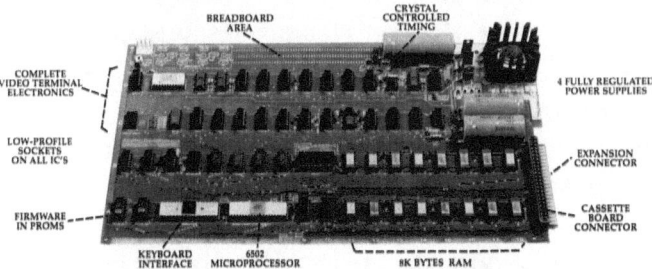

APPLE Computer Company • 770 Welch Rd., Palo Alto, CA 94304 • (415) 326-4248
OCTOBER 1976   CIRCLE NO. 7 ON INQUIRY CARD   INTERFACE AGE 11

Advertisement for the Apple-1

1979 CE – **Idi Amin Deposed**

Ugandan dictator Idi Amin, whose reign of terror killed between 100,000 and 500,000 people, was forced to flee into exile on April 11, 1979, as a result of defeats and defections of his forces in the Uganda-Tanzania War. He was given sanctuary in Saudi Arabia, where his lived until his death in 2003.

1987 CE – **London Agreement Signed**

In a secret London meeting, King Hussein of Jordan and Israeli Foreign Affairs Minister Shimon Peres (later President of Israel) negotiated a framework for an international peace conference to resolve the Arab-Israeli conflict, signing it on April 11, 1987. Prime Minister Yitzhak Shamir rejected the agreement and blocked the peace conference.

1993 CE – **Easter Prison Riot**

On Easter Sunday, April 11, 1993, a riot broke out in the maximum security Southern Ohio Correctional Facility, involving grievances about prison conditions. Prisoners took over the facility for ten days; nine inmates and one guard died.

2011 CE – **Minsk Metro Bombing**

On April 11, 2011, a bombing at the central station on the Minsk Metro in Belarus killed 15 and injured 200. The perpetrators were caught and executed, but their motives remain unclear to this day.

Who Was Born on April 11?

Acting and Film

Dakota Blue Richards (April 11, 1994 —)

Richards is known for her role as the lead character Lyra in the film *The Golden Compass*.

Stephanie Pratt (April 11, 1986 —)

Reality TV star Pratt is known for her role on *The Hills*.

Brett Claywell (April 11, 1978 —)

Claywell played Tim Smith on *One Tree Hill* and Kyle Lewis on *One Life to Live*.

Zöe Lucker (April 11, 1974 —)

English actress Lucker is known for her featured roles on *Footballers' Wives*, *EastEnders*, and *Waterloo Road*.

Tricia Helfer
(April 11, 1974 —)

Helfer is best known for her role as a Cylon in the remake of the *Battlestar Galactica* TV series, and as a model appeared in ad campaigns for Ralph Lauren, Versace, and Giorgio Armani.

Tricia Helfer

Anton Glanzelius (April 11, 1974 —)

Swedish actor Glanzelius is primarily known for his starring role in the 1985 film *My Life as a Dog*.

Jennifer Esposito (April 11, 1973 —)

Actress Jennifer Esposito appeared in such films as *I Still Know What You Did Last Summer* and *Crash*, and in TV shows including *Spin City* and *Samantha Who?*

Mason Reese (April 11, 1965 —)

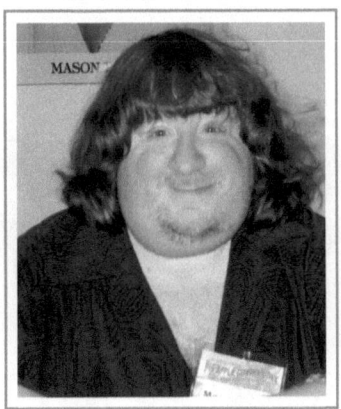

As a child actor in the 1970s, Reese (right) was known for his distinctive appearance and roles in television commercials for such products as Underwood Deviled Ham, Post Raisin Bran, and Dunkin' Donuts' "donut holes."

Meshach Taylor (April 11, 1947 —)

Taylor was nominated for an Emmy for his role on the CBS sitcom *Designing Women* and played the principal on the Nickelodeon sitcom *Ned's Declassified School Survival Guide.*

Peter Riegert (April 11, 1947 —)

Riegert is known for playing Boon in *Animal House* and Assemblyman Zellman on *The Sopranos.*

John Milius (April 11, 1944 —)

Screenwriter, director, and producer John Milius wrote the first two *Dirty Harry* films, *Apocalypse Now, Conan the Barbarian,* and *Red Dawn,* directing the latter two.

Louise Lasser
(April 11, 1939 —)

Actress Louise Lasser (left) is known for her starring role on the soap opera parody *Mary Hartman, Mary Hartman,* and for her appearances in several films made by her former husband Woody Allen.

Joel Grey (April 11, 1932 —)

Actor, singer, and dancer Joel Grey won the Academy Award, the Tony, and the Golden Globe. He is particularly known for his role in the stage and film version of *Cabaret.*

Johnny Sheffield (April 11, 1931 — October 15, 2010)

Child star Johnny Sheffield was best known for playing "Boy" in the Johnny Weissmuller *Tarzan* films. In the film *Knute Rockne, All American,* he played the lead character as a child, and starred in the *Bomba, the Jungle Boy* films.

He left show business in the late 1950s and worked in farming, real estate, and construction.

Johnny Sheffield (right) with Johnny Weissmuller in 1939's *Tarzan Finds a Son!*

Arts and Literature

Peter O'Donnell (April 11, 1920 — May 3, 2010)

O'Donnell created the book and comics character *Modesty Blaise,* and under the pseudonym Madeline Brent won the 1978 Romantic Novel of the Year Award for *Merlin's Keep.*

David Westheimer (April 11, 1917 — November 8, 2005)

Westheimer is best known as the author of the 1964 novel *Von Ryan's Express*, adapted into a movie starring Frank Sinatra. During World War II, he was a navigator on a B-24, shot down over Italy, and imprisoned in Stalag Luft III.

Leo Rosten (April 11, 1908 — February 19, 1997)

Screenwriter and novelist Leo Rosten is best known for the *H*Y*M*A*N K*A*P*L*A*N* stories, for his book *The Joys of Yiddish*, and for such films as *Captain Newman, M.D.* and *The Dark Corner*. He often wrote under the pseudonym Leonard Q. Ross.

Dale Messick (April 11, 1906 — April 5, 2005)

Comic strip artist Dale Messick created *Brenda Starr, Reporter*, which ran nationwide in over 250 newspapers.

Cover of newspaper strip anthology of *Brenda Starr, Reporter*, by Dale Messick

Fashion

Alessandra Ambrosio (April 11, 1981 —)

Portuguese supermodel Ambrosio is best known as a Victoria's Secret Angel and spokesmodel for their "Pink" line.

Oleg Cassini (April 11, 1913 — March 17,2 006)

Oleg Cassini is best known as the "Secretary of Style" who designed numerous dresses for First Lady Jacqueline Kennedy. He was a pioneer and innovator in designer licensing, putting his name on luggage, cosmetics, and even the 1974/75 AMC Matador Coupé automobile.

Music

Joss Stone (April 11, 1987 —)

British soul singer and actress Stone received three Grammy nominations (one win) and was the youngest British female singer to have her first album reach #1 on the UK Albums Chart. She played Anne of Cleves in the cable TV series *The Tudors*.

Lights (April 11, 1987 —)

Electropop musician Lights (Valerie Poxleitner) won the 2009 Juno Award for New Artist of the Year.

Danja (April 11, 1982 —)

Hip hop record producer Danja (Floyd Hills) produced numerous hits for such acts as Timbaland, Britney Spears, Madonna, Justin Timberlake, and Mariah Carey.

Nick LaRocca (April 11, 1889 — February 22, 1961)

Cornetist and trumpeter Nick LaRocca led the Original Dixieland Jazz Band, and played on the first jazz recording, 1917's "Livery Stable Blues." He is best known for composing the jazz standard "Tiger Rag."

1918 promotional card for the Original Dixieland Jazz Band. From left to right, Tony Spargo (drums), Daddy Edwards (trombone), **Nick LaRocca (cornet)**, Larry Shields (clarinet), Henry Ragas (piano)

Newsmakers and Broadcasters

Jeremy Clarkson (April 11, 1960 —)

English broadcaster and journalist Clarkson is best known for his role on the BBC series *Top Gear*.

Ana María Polo (April 11, 1958 —)

Cuban-American lawyer Polo is the judge on the Spanish-language court show *Caso Cerrado* on Telemundo.

Richard "The Iceman" Kuklinski (April 11, 1935 — March 5, 2006)

Serial killer Richard Kuklinski turned his hobby into a career by becoming a Mafia contract killer for the Five Families. He was arrested in 1986, convicted of five murders, and died in prison.

Tony Brown (April 11, 1933 —)

Journalist Brown is best known for his syndicated television series, *Tony Brown's Journal*.

Anton LaVey (April 11, 1930 — October 29, 1997)

Occultist and musician Anton LaVey (right) wrote *The Satanic Bible* and founded the Church of Satan.

Politics and Law

Michael Deaver (April 11, 1938 — August 18, 2007)

Deaver was Deputy Chief of Staff to President Ronald Reagan. He was convicted of perjury for lying to a Congressional committee about his lobbying activities following his departure from the White House and fined $100,000.

Nicholas F. Brady (April 11, 1930 —)

Former New Jersey Senator Nicholas Brady was Secretary of the Treasury under Presidents Ronald Reagan and George H. W. Bush, and developed the Brady Plan to provide support to developing countries defaulting on their international debt.

Ethel Kennedy (April 11, 1928 —)

Ethel Kennedy is the widow of former Senator and Attorney General Robert F. Kennedy. The couple had 11 children.

Kasturba Mohandas Gandhi (April 11, 1869 — February 22, 1944)

Kasturba Gandhi was the wife of Mahatma Gandhi, and a political activist in her own right, frequently taking her husband's place when he was under arrest.

Dean Acheson
(April 11, 1893 — October 12, 1971)

Secretary of State in the Truman Administration, Acheson (left) was an important player in defining American Cold War policy. He helped design the Marshall Plan, the Truman Doctrine, and NATO. He persuaded Truman to intervene in the Korean War and aid French forces in Indochina, and advised JFK during the Cuban Missile Crisis.

Charles Evans Hughes (April 11, 1862 — August 27, 1948)

Charles Evans Hughes was the 11th Chief Justice of the U.S. Supreme Court, the Republican candidate in the 1916 Presidential election (losing to Woodrow Wilson), the Secretary of State, and the Governor of New York.

Edward Everett (April 11, 1794 — January 15, 1865)

Congressman, Massachusetts governor, and Secretary of State Edward Everett was a well-known orator of the period — but his two-hour speech at the 1863 dedication ceremony for the Gettysburg National Cemetery paled before President Abraham Lincoln's two-minute Gettysburg Address.

Science, Math and Medicine

Sir Andrew Wiles (April 11, 1953 —)

Mathematician Wiles is best known for proving Fermat's Last Theorem, listed in the Guinness Book of World Records as "most difficult math problem."

Percy Lavon Julian (April 11, 1899 — April 19, 1975)

Percy Lavon Julian (right) was one of the first African-Americans to receive a doctorate in chemistry. A pioneer in the chemical synthesis of medicinal drugs from plants, he received more than 130 chemical patents and developed techniques that reduced the cost of manufacturing a number of important drugs. He was the first African-American chemist and only the second African-American scientist inducted into the National Academy of Science.

James Parkinson (April 11, 1755 — December 21, 1824)

Surgeon, geologist, paleontologist, and political activist James Parkinson wrote the 1817 An Essay on the Shaking Palsy, making him the first to describe formally the disease that bears his name: Parkinson's disease.

Sports

Lena Schöneborn (April 11, 1986 —)

Pentathlete Schöneborn won the gold at the 2008 Summer Olympics.

Jennifer Heil (April 11, 1983 —)

Canadian freestyle skier Heil won a gold medal at the 2006 Winter Olympics and a silver at the 2010 Winter Olympics. She holds the world championship in dual moguls.

Alexandre Burrows (April 11, 1981 —)

NHL right winger Burrows began with the Vancouver Canucks in 2005 after a ball hockey career in which he was named International Ball Hockey Player of the Year and was inducted into both the Canadian and International Ball Hockey Hall of Fame.

Mark Teixeria (April 11, 1980 —)

New York Yankee Teixeria won five Gold Glove Awards and three Silver Slugger Awards and holds the all-time MLB record for most games with a home run from both sides of the plate.

Mark Teixeria

Josh Hancock (April 11, 1978 — April 29, 2007)

MLB pitcher Hancock played for four different teams beginning in 2002, and was killed in a car crash during the 2007 season.

Trot Nixon (April 11, 1974 —)

Right fielder Nixon played professionally from 1996 through 2008 for several teams, primarily the Boston Red Sox.

Jason Varitek (April 11, 1972 —)

Boston Red Sox catcher Varitek was a three-time All-Star and Gold Glove Award winner as catcher and received a Silver Slugger Award, and became captain of the Red Sox in 2004.

Trevor Linden (April 11, 1970 —)

Linden (below) played 19 seasons in the National Hockey League and served as president of the players association during the 2004-05 NHL lockout.

Bret Saberhagen (April 11, 1964 —)

MLB pitcher Saberhagen won the Gold Glove Award, two Cy Young Awards, and a World Series MVP with the Kansas City Royals, New York Mets, Colorado Rockies, and Boston Red Sox.

Richard Sévigny (April 11, 1957 —)

Hockey goaltender Sévigny played for the Montreal Canadiens and the Quebec Nordiques.

Micheal Ray Richardson (April 11, 1955 —)

Former NBA player Micheal Ray Richardson achieved over 8,200 points in his eight year career, and was banned from the league after repeated violations of its drug policy.

Edwin Pope (April 11, 1928 —)

Award-winning Miami *Herald* sportswriter Edwin Pope has been called "the best writer of sports in America."

George J. Maloof, Sr. (April 11, 1923 — November 29, 1980)

Businessman George Maloof was an owner of the Houston Rockets.

Who Died on April 11?

Arts and Literature

Kurt Vonnegut (November 11, 1922 — April 11, 2007)

Vonnegut was known for his many novels including *Slaughterhouse-Five, Player Piano, Cat's Cradle, Breakfast of Champions,* and *God Bless You, Mr. Rosewater.*

William H. Armstrong (September 14, 1911 — April 11, 1999)

Children's author Armstrong won the Newbery Medal for his 1969 novel *Sounder.*

Erskine Caldwell (December 17, 1903 — April 11, 1987)

Caldwell's well-known novels about poverty and racism in the American south include *Tobacco Road* and *God's Little Acre,* both made into films.

John O'Hara (January 31, 1905 — April 11, 1970)

Best-selling novelist John O'Hara is known for such works as *Appointment in Samarra* and *BUtterfield 8.*

Richard Harding Davis (April 18, 1864 — April 11, 1916)

War correspondent Richard Davis helped create the career of Theodore Roosevelt by his promotion of the Rough Riders, and had numerous adventures, including being arrested as a spy by the Germans during World War I. Considered the model for the "Gibson man," the equivalent to the Gibson Girl, his dashing appearance is credited with making the clean-shaven look popular among men.

Richard Harding Davis

Francis P. Church (February 22, 1839 — April 11, 1906)

Magazine and newspaper publisher and editor Francis P. Church co-founded *The Army and Navy Journal* and *Galaxy* magazine (later merged with the *Atlantic Monthly*). He is best known today for an editorial he wrote for his brother's newspaper, the New York *Sun*, entitled "Yes, Virginia, There Is a Santa Claus."

Francisco González Bocanegra (January 8, 1824 — April 11, 1861)

Poet Bocanegra wrote the lyrics to the Mexican National Anthem.

Entertainment and Music

June Pointer (November 30, 1953 — April 11, 2006)

June Pointer was a founder and lead singer of The Pointer Sisters.

Harry Secombe (September 8, 1921 — April 11, 2001)

Welsh comedian Sir Harry Secombe was best known for playing Neddie Seagoon in the BBC radio series *The Goon Show.*

James Brown

(March 22, 1920 — April 11, 1992)

Actor James E. Brown (left) was best known for his role as Lieutenant Rip Masters in the 1950s television series *The Adventures of Rin-Tin-Tin*. He appeared in more than forty films as well as in the TV series *Dallas* as Detective Harry McSween, an ally of J. R. Ewing.

Dolores del Río (August 3, 1905 — April 11, 1983)

Legendary Mexican actress Dolores del Río was one of the few silent screen stars to make the transition to talkies. Her Hollywood films include *Flying Down to Rio* and *Madame Du Barry*. She returned to Mexico and became the most important star of the Golden Age of Mexican cinema, remembered particularly for her 1943 classic *Maria Candelaria*.

Dolores del Río

James A. Bailey
(July 4, 1847 — April 11, 1906)

Circus ringmaster James Bailey (right) famously partnered with impressario P. T. Barnum to form Barnum and Bailey's Circus, later merged with Ringling Brothers to become the "The Greatest Show on Earth."

Military

Merlin German (November 15, 1985 — April 11, 2008)

Marine Sergeant Merlin German became known as the "Miracle Marine" for his recovery from a roadside bomb blast in Iraq.

Ronald Speirs (April 20, 1920 — April 11, 2007)

As an officer with the 506th Parachute Infantry Regiment, Speirs was featured in the book and miniseries *Band of Brothers*, played by Matthew Settle in the latter.

Thomas Farrell (December 3, 1891 — April 11, 1967)

Major General Thomas Farrell was Deputy Commanding General of the Manhattan Project and supervised the bombings of Hiroshima and Nagasaki from the 509th Composite Group base on the island of Tinian.

Newsmakers

Jessica Dubroff (May 5, 1988 — April 11, 1996)

Seven-year old pilot trainee Jessica Dubroff died, along with her father and flight instructor, when her single-engine Cessna crashed after takeoff during an attempt to set a record for the youngest person to fly across the United States.

Francisco González Bocanegra (January 8, 1824 — April 11, 1861)

Poet Bocanegra wrote the lyrics to the Mexican National Anthem.

Louise Peete (September 20, 1880 — April 11, 1947)

Serial killer Louise Peete killed at least three husbands along with other wealthy people. She was convicted of murder and executed in 1947.

The Elephant Man (August 5, 1862 — April 11, 1890)

Joseph Merrick (next page) was an Englishman of the Victorian Era who suffered from severe deformities (medical authorities are unsure, but the current theory is that he had some combination of neurofibromatosis type I and Proteus syndrome) and who was exhibited as a human curiosity under the name of the Elephant Man.

After being robbed by his manager, he was taken in by physician Frederick Treves, who arranged for him to live at the London Hospital for the rest of his life. Merrick became well known in London society and was friendly with such figures as Alexandra, Princess of Wales. His story was told in a Broadway play and a film by David Lynch, both titled *The Elephant Man.*

Politics

Ahmed Ben Bella (أحمد بن بلّة) (December 25, 1916 — April 11, 2012)

Ben Bella was the first president of Algeria following its independence from France.

Enver Hoxha (October 16, 1908 — April 11, 1985)

Hoxha was Communist dictator of Albania from 1944 to his death.

Joseph Merrick, The Elephant Man

Sir Thomas Wyatt the Younger (1521 — April 11, 1554)

English rebel Thomas Wyatt led "Wyatt's Rebellion," an unsuccessful attempt to stop the marriage of Queen Mary I of England ("Bloody Mary") to King Phillip II of Spain, which was strongly unpopular in England. He was captured and executed at the Tower of London.

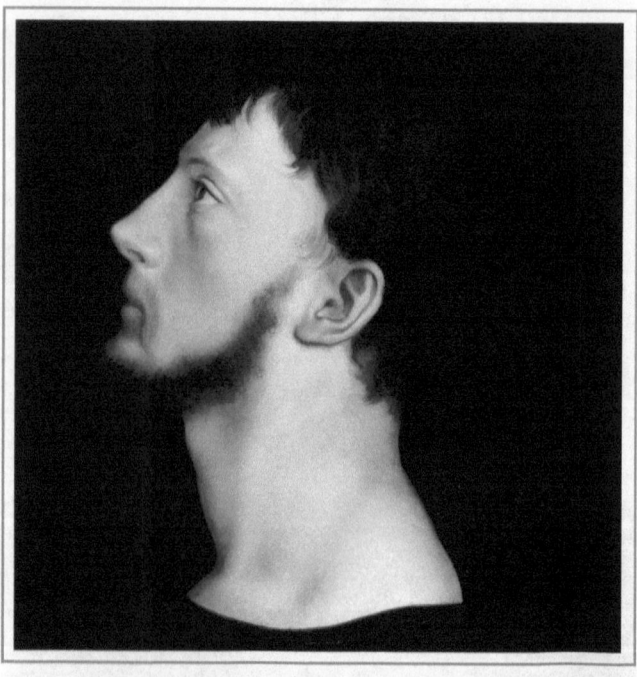

Sir Thoms Wyatt the Younger by Hans Holbein the Younger

Llywelyn the Great (c. 1172 — April 11, 1240)

Llywelyn ap Iorwerth was Prince of Gwynedd in north Wales and *de facto* ruler of the country for 40 years. He allied with the barons who forced King John to sign the Magna Carta.

Religion

Saint Gemma Galgani (March 12, 1878 — April 11, 1903)

Italian mystic Gemma Galgani was known as the "Daughter of Passion" for her stigmata corresponding to the crucifixion wounds of Jesus. She was beatified in 1933 and canonized in 1940. She is the patron saint of students and pharmacists, and revered particularly in Italy and Latin America.

Edward Wightman (c. 1580 — April 11, 1612)

Wightman, an Anabaptist, was the last person to be burned at the stake for heresy in England.

Science

Primo Levi (July 31, 1919 — April 11, 1987)

Italian Jewish chemist and writer Levi's best known works include *If This Is a Man* about his captivity in the Auschwitz concentration camp, and *The Periodic Table*, named by the Royal Institution of Great Britain as the "best science book ever written."

Ukichiro Nakaya (中谷 宇吉郎) (July 4, 1900 — April 11, 1962)

Japanese physicist Ukichiro Nakaya is credited with making the first artificial snowflakes.

Luther Burbank (March 7, 1849 — April 11, 1926)

Botanist Luther Burbank (next page), known as the "Wizard of Horticulture," developed more than 800 strains and varieties of plants, including the Elberta Peach, the Santa Rosa Plum, and the Russet Burbank Potato.

Sports

Walker Cooper (January 8, 1915— April 11, 1991)

MLB catcher Cooper played for six National League teams from 1940 to 1957 and was known as one of the top catchers in baseball during his career.

George Poage (November 6, 1880 — April 11, 1962)

Poage was the first African-American athlete to win an Olympic medal, taking the bronze in the 200 meter and 400 meter hurdles in the 1904 St. Louis Olympic Games.

Luther Burbank

Kid Nichols (March 7, 1849 — April 11, 1926)

Baseball hall of famer Kid Nichols played fifteen seasons for the Boston Beaneaters, the St. Louis Cardinals, and the Philadelphia Phillies, and is the youngest pitcher to join the "300 Win Club."

Kid Nichols

April
The Fourth Month

"I love the season well
When forest glades are teeming with bright forms,
Nor dark and many-folded clouds foretell
The coming on of storms."

— *"An April Day," Henry Wadsworth Longfellow*

The origin of the name "April" (Latin: *Aprilis*) for the fourth month of the year is uncertain. Some say that it comes from the Latin verb *aperire*, meaning "to open," a reference to springtime. A similar word in Greek, ἄνοιξις (*anoixis*), meaning "opening" also refers to spring.

On the other hand, the Romans named many months after their gods, such as "January" for Janus and "March" (*Martius*) for Mars. The month of April was sacred to the goddess Venus (*Aphrodite* in Greek), and thus some think that April refers to her.

The fairy tale collector Jacob Grimm suggested that April came from the Etruscan name *Apru*, and believed that an Etruscan god or hero of that name gave rise to the month.

As the original Roman calendar started its new year in March, April was originally the second month of the year. It's uncertain when the Romans switched the new year to January, but it may have been as late as 153 BCE.

April is the springtime month in the northern hemisphere and fall in the southern hemisphere; October is its opposite. It's one of only four calendar months with thirty days. Originally, April had only 29 days, but the calendar reforms of Julius Caesar (the Julian Calendar) added the 30th day.

The first day of April and the first day of July always fall on the same day of the week; in leap years the first of January also falls on the same weekday as the first of April. In all years, the last day of April and the last day of December fall on the same wekday.

April in Other Cultures

The Anglo-Saxons called April *Oster-monath*, sometimes spelled *Eostur-monath*, named for the goddess *Eostre*. The Venerable Bede, a monk who wrote the first history of the English people, argued that Eostur was the root of the word Easter.

In China, the Emperor and princes of the blood would symbolically plow the earth to get ready for the planting season. This took place in their third month, sān yuè (三月), which most often overlaps with April in their traditional lunisolar calendar.

In Finland, March is called *huhtikuu* (burnwood month), representing the clearing of farmland. In Slovene, the traditional name is *mali traven* (the months when plants start growing). In Hebrew, Arabic, and modern Turkish, the month of *Nisan* (Hebrew: נִיסָן ; Arabic: نيسان) overlaps March and April. It comes from a Sumerian word, *nisag*, meaning "first fruits."

April Symbols

Birthstone: Diamond

Birth Flowers: Daisy and Sweet Pea

Daisy   Sweet Pea

April Events

Honorary Months

Presidents, Congresses, and nations around the world issue proclamations recognizing particular months to honor certain causes. These events generally fall in April. (All US unless otherwise noted.)

- Autism Awareness Month
- Confederate History Month (southern United States)
- Financial Literacy Month
- Jazz Appreciation Month
- National Arab-American Heritage Month
- National Child Abuse Prevention Month
- National Poetry Month
- Parkinson's Disease Awareness Month (International)

Moveable and Multi-Day Events

Some events take place over a specific week or time period. Start and finish dates may vary from year to year. Some events occur on different days each year (such as "fourth Saturday of a month"). The events of Easter season are part of this category, but the number of the events are such that Easter receives its own separate section.

International Trombone Week

Sponsored by the International Trombone Association, International Trombone Week took place on April 7-14 in 2013, and April 1-15 in 2012. Numerous recitals, concerts, and symposia take place around the world celebrating the trombone. (www.trombone.net)

Passover (פסח) (Judaism, Samaritanism, Saint Thomas Christians)

Passover commemorates the liberation of the Israelites from slavery in ancient Egypt around 3,300 years ago. Its story is told in the Biblical book of Exodus, which is part of both the Jewish and Samaritan Torahs and the Christian Old Testament. Exodus tells how God inflicted ten plagues upon the ancient Egyptians before the Pharaoh would release its slaves. The tenth plague killed every Egyptian first-born child. Israelites marked the doorposts of their homes with the blood of a spring lamb so that the spirit of the Lord would "pass over" the first-born in those homes. Passover is celebrated by Jews in a festive ritual dinner known as a Seder and by Samaritans with an animal sacrifice on Mount Gerizim.

For most celebrants, Passover begins on the 15th day of Nisan and ends on the 21st of Nisan in Israel and on the 22nd of Nisan outside of Israel. The earliest dates for Passover are between March 21 and March 27 (or 28), and the latest dates fall between April 20 and April 26 (or 27).

Opening Day (Major League Baseball)

Major League Baseball generally begins its annual season on the first Monday in April (although it has been moved to different days to keep the World Series from extending into November).

President Woodrow Wilson throws the Opening Day pitch, 1916

Easter Events

La crucifixión by El Greco

Easter Season

The Christian holiday of Easter in Western Christianity is held on the first Sunday after the Paschal Full Moon following the March equinox, which is officially set at March 21 by church reckoning. Easter itself can therefore occur as early as March 22 and as late as April 25, but occurs most often in April. In Eastern Christianity, which uses the Julian calendar, Easter occurs between April 4 and May 8. This also sets the date for the various events that lead up to Easter, most importantly the events of Holy Week.

Passion Sunday

The fifth Sunday of the Christian season of Lent is known as Passion Sunday in various Protestant denominations and by some traditionalist Catholics. Sometimes, the sixth Sunday of Lent is referred to as Passion Sunday, but it is more commonly known as Palm Sunday.

Passion Sunday starts the two-week Passiontide, which ends on Holy Saturday, the day before Easter, commemorating the day that Jesus's body was laid in the tomb. The fifth Sunday of Lent can occur as early as March 8 (though the next time it will be that early is in 2285 CE), and as late as April 11.

Palm Sunday

The moveable feast of Palm Sunday commemorates the triumphant entry of Jesus into Jerusalem, an event mentioned in all four gospels. In many Christian churches, palm leaves are distributed to the worshippers. The earliest date for Palm Sunday is March 15, and the latest is April 18.

Maundy Thursday

The Thursday before Easter is Maundy Thursday, when the Last Supper took place. The earliest day it can occur is March 19, and the latest is April 22.

Good Friday

Good Friday, observed during Holy Week on the Friday preceding Easter Sunday, commemorates the crucifixion of Jesus and his death at Calvary. The earliest day it can occur is March 20, and the latest is April 23.

Holy Saturday

Sometimes called Easter Eve or Black Saturday, Holy Saturday commemorates the day in which Jesus's body lay in the tomb. Some mistakenly refer to this day as "Easter Saturday," but that properly describes the Saturday following Easter, the last day of Easter Week. The earliest it can occur is March 21, and the latest is April 24.

Easter Eggs

Easter

Easter celebrates the resurrection of Jesus Christ on the third day after his crucifixion.

In the liturgical calendar, Easter follows the season of Lent, and begins the period known as Eastertide, which ends on Pentecost Sunday. Easter is observed religiously in a morning service.

In the U.S., it's also common to decorate Easter eggs and make Easter baskets of eggs and candy, often with the Easter bunny as a symbol. The White House traditionally hosts an egg hunt, and many communities have Easter parades.

Easter customs around the world include bonfires (Cyprus, western Sweden), men spanking women with a ceremonial whip (Czech Republic and Slovakia), egg fighting (Bulgaria), cross-country skiing and reading murder mysteries (Norway), and children dressed as witches collecting candy door-to-door (other Nordic countries).

Easter Monday

In some Roman Catholic and Eastern Orthodox cultures, the Monday after Easter is celebrated as a holiday.

It is also known in some countries as **Egg Nyte**, featuring egg rolling competitions and dousing other people with water that had been blessed with holy water the previous day at mass.

Easter Monday is also celebrated as **Family Day** in South Africa. In Guyana, people fly kites that were made on Holy Saturday. In Portugal, it is known as the **Anjo (Ivy) Festival**, in which people picnic in the countryside.

Śmigus-Dyngus (Poland, Hungary, Czech Republic, Slovakia)

The Monday after Easter in Poland and in the Polish diaspora is known as *Śmigus-Dyngus*, or simply Dyngus Day in the US. Boys throw water over girls they like and spank them with pussy willows. Girls avoid getting wet by giving boys "ransoms" of painted eggs.

Easter Week (Western Christianity)
Bright Week (Eastern Christianity)

The period from Easter Sunday to the following Saturday is known as **Easter Week**. In both Western and Eastern Christianity (where it's known as **Bright Week**), the resurrection continues to be celebrated in church services. **Easter Tuesday** is a public holiday in the Australian state of Tasmania. Because of the difference in the calculation of the date of Easter, Easter Week and Bright Week happen on different weeks each year.

A Bright Week procession

March Zodiac Signs

From the perspective of someone on Earth, the Sun appears to move through the sky throughout the year, along a path astronomers call the ecliptic plane. The ecliptic plane is divided into twelve constellations, known as the zodiac, based on traditionally observed patterns of stars. On your birthday, you can't see your constellation, because it's part of the daytime sky.

The zodiac was first developed by Babylonian astronomers about 2,500 years ago. Because they were unaware that the Earth wobbles like a spinning top (a motion known as *precession*), they didn't make allowance for the fact that the Sun's path through the zodiac changes over time.

That means there are now two sets of dates for your birth sign. The *tropical* dates are the original Babylonian dates; the *siderial* dates tell you where the Sun actually appears as it moves along its annual path.

In siderial reckoning, April 11 is in Pisces, but in tropical astrology, April 11 is in Aries.

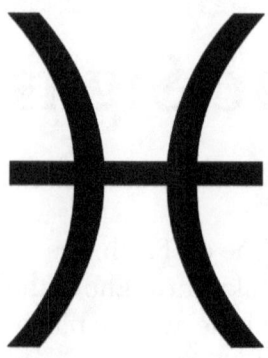

Pisces

Tropical February 20 to March 20

Siderial March 15 to April 14

In the Roman legend of Venus and her son Cupid, they escaped the clutches of Typhon, known as the "father of all monsters," by transforming into fish and tying themselves together with rope. That's why the name Pisces is plural for fish. The constellation appears as a somewhat ragged "V" shape, representing the rope, with the "fish" located at the two rope ends.

In astrology, Pisces is a water sign, compatible with the other water signs Cancer and Scorpio, as well as with the earth signs Taurus, Virgo, and Capricorn. Pisceans are supposed to be imaginative, compassionate, unworldly, secretive, and escapist.

Aries

Tropical March 21 to April 19

Siderial April 15 to May 15

In Greek mythology, Aries is a ram with golden wings and golden wool who rescued the twins Phrixus and Helle from certain death. Although Helle died in the rescue attempt, the grateful Phrixus sacrificed the ram to Zeus. The golden fleece from the sacrificed ram played a prominent part in the later myth of Jason and the Argonauts.

In astrology, Aries, a fire sign, is compatible with the other fire signs of Gemini, Leo, and Sagittarius, and to a lesser extent with air signs Scorpio and Libra. Arians are supposed to be adventurous, enthusiastic, quick-tempered, and impulsive.

Illustration by Edward Penfield

What Day of the Week is April 11?

On what day of the week does April 11 fall?

Surprisingly, this isn't an easy question. Because the calendar year is 365 days long (366 in leap years), it doesn't divide evenly by the seven days of the week.

Also, the Earth goes around the Sun in about 365-1/4 days, so a calendar tends to drift over time. That's why the same date falls on different weekdays in different years.

This is made even more complicated by a change in calendars that took place in 1582. Our modern calendar has its roots in ancient Rome, in a calendar reform conducted by Julius Caesar. Caesar commissioned mathematicians to attack the problem, and came up with the idea of *leap years*, and thus standardized the calendar for centuries to come. This was called the *Julian calendar.*

Over time, however, the small errors in Caesar's calculation compounded. That's why Pope Gregory XIII commissioned the *Gregorian calendar,* used in most of the world today. Some countries converted in 1582, when the calendar was first developed;

some converted later; other still haven't changed.

Gregorian and Julian aren't the only types of calendars. The Hebrew year, the Islamic year, and many other calendars are used in different parts of the world and among different people.

You can convert Gregorian dates to other calendars, including the Hebrew calendar, the Islamic calendar, and even the Mayan calendar by visiting the Fourmilab Calendar Converter at http://www.fourmilab.ch/documents/calendar/.

Chinese calendar systems are quite complex and have changed several times; a full discussion is far beyond the scope of this book. If you're interested, you can find information here: http://www.hermetic.ch/cal_stud/chinese_cal.htm.

A 50-year brass perpetual calendar.

Copyright, Credit, and Contact

Follow Us

Our blog Dobson's Improbable History features short articles on events and people associated with each day, and updates several times each week. Get the latest on Twitter @SidewiseThinker.

Contact Us

Find an error or a format problem? Want information about the series, about us, or about when the volume for your special day might be available? Please email us at editor@timespinnerpress.com.

On Dates

Historians use "CE" (Common Era) and "BCE" (Before the Common Era) instead of the more common "AD" (*Anno Domini*, or Year of Our Lord) and "BC" (Before Christ), reflecting the fact that the year-numbering system established by the Gregorian calendar is used throughout the world in many countries not culturally Christian. The CE/BCE designation dates back to at least 1708, and have been adopted as a standard by the United Nations and the Universal Postal Union. Because this series of books covers events and people of all nations and cultures, we use the CE/BCE terms.

The abbreviation "O.S." on some dates refers to the fact that the Russian Empire did not switch from the Julian to the Gregorian calendar at the same time as the rest of Europe, and therefore some figures and events have two dates.

People and events whose original names are not in the Western alphabet have their native names (where possible) in the appropriate script shown in parenthesis. If you are using an e-reader to access an electronic version of this book, all characters don't always display on all devices.

Sources and Art Credits

We owe a great debt to Wikipedia, which is our first stop for research. We attempt to make independent confirmation of all important dates and facts through a variety of other sources. Other sources we frequently use include the Library of Congress, "on this day" listings from *Encyclopedia Britannica*, the New York *Times*, and the BBC, and, of course, the always-useful Google.

All art and photographs are either in the public domain, used under a Creative Commons license, or with a "fair use" justification, and most frequently come from Wikimedia Commons and the Library of Congress Prints and Photographs Division.

Attribution is provided where requested by the copyright owner or when of historical significance, listed below. For information about any particular illustration of photograph, please contact us.

- The cover illustration is from an official NASA photograph. As a work of the U.S. federal government, it is in the public domain.

- The illustration of the month of March used on the back cover and in the interior is from the French Gothic illuminated manuscript *Les Très Riches Heures du duc de Berry* by the Limbourg Brothers, Jean Colombe, and an intermediate painter whose name is lost to history. It is in the public domain because its copyright has expired.

- The portrait of William and Mary is part of the 18th century *Ceiling of the Painted Hall* by Sir James Thornhill, photograph taken by James Brittain. It is in the public domain because its copyright has expired.

- The portrait of Napoléon Bonaparte by Paul Delaroche was painted around 1840 and is in the public domain because its copyright has expired.

- The photograph of a Buchenwald inmate identifying a Nazi guard is in the public domain as an image created by the U.S. federal government.

- The photograph of LBJ signing the Civil Rights Act of 1968 is in the public domain as an image created by the U.S. federal government.

- The advertisement for the Apple-1 Computer appeared in the October 1976 issue of *Computer Age* magazine. It is in the public domain because it was published in the U.S. between 1923 and 1977 without a copyright notice.

- The photograph of Tricia Helfer at the 2007 Scream Awards was taken by pinguino k and is used here under the CC BY-SA 2.0 license.

- The 2008 photograph of Mason Reese at the Big Apple Convention was taken by Nightscream and is used here under the CC BY-SA 3.0 license.

- The 1976 publicity photograph of Louise Lasser on *Saturday*

in size and unsuitable for the production of counterfeit materials. Its sole purpose is to identify the historical figure described here, and no free alternative is known to exist.

- The publicity photograph of Dolores del Río is in the public domain because it was published in the U.S. between 1923 and 1977 without a copyright notice. It was taken by studio photographer Ernest A. Bachrach.

- The 1895 portrait of James A. Bailey is in the public domain because its copyright is expired. The image is from the collection of the Boston Public Library.

- The author of the 1889 photograph of Joseph Merrick is unknown. The image is in the public domain because its copyright has expired.

- The painting of Thomas Wyatt is by Hans Holbein the Younger c. 1540 and is in the public domain because its copyright has expired.

- The photograph of Luther Burbank is from the September 1908 issue of *Overland Monthly,* and is in the public domain because its copyright has expired.

- The 1905 photograph of Kid Nichols is in the public domain because its copyright has expired.

- The photograph of two diamonds grown by Washington Diamonds was taken by Inbai-Tania Studio, and is used here under the CC BY-SA 3.0 license.

- The photograph of a daisy (*Bellis perennis*) was taken by André Karwath and is used here under the CC BY-SA 2.5 license.

- The photograph of President Woodrow Wilson throwing the ball on the opening day of baseball season 1916 is a press photograph from the National Photo Company Collection, part of the Library of Congress Prints and Photographs Division, and is in the public domain because it was published prior to January 1, 1923.

- The painting *La crucifixión* by El Greco is located in the Museo del Prado. It is in the public domain because its copyright has expired.

- The photograph of Czechoslovakian Easter eggs was taken by Jan Kameníček, who has released the image into the public domain.

- The 1988 photograph of a Bright Week procession is by George Rassasphore and is used here under the CC BY-SA 1.0 license.

- The photograph of the 1906 automobile calendar by Edward Penfield is from the Library of Congress Prints and Photographs Division, and is in the public domain because it was published prior to January 1, 1923.

- The 50-year perpetual calendar photograph is in the public domain.

License Description and Terms

Aside from material purely in the public domain, photographs and other material in this book are used under specific licenses permitting free use, usually with attribution. For full text and terms of these licenses, click or enter the appropriate links below.

Creative Commons Attribution-Share Alike 3.0 Generic (CC BY-SA 3.0): http://creativecommons.org/licenses/by-sa/3.0/

Creative Commons Attribution-Share Alike 2.5 Generic (CC BY-SA 2.5): http://creativecommons.org/licenses/by-sa/2.5/deed.en

Creative Commons Attribution-Share Alike 2.0 Generic (CC BY-SA 2.0): http://creativecommons.org/licenses/by/2.0/deed.en

Creative Commons Attribution-Share Alike 1.0 Generic (CC BY-SA 1.0): http://creativecommons.org/licenses/by-sa/1.0/deed.en

GNU Free Documentation License (GFDL): http://en.wikipedia.org/wiki/Wikipedia:Text_of_the_GNU_Free_Documentation_License

9 7 8 1 4 8 4 0 3 4 0 5 7